Excel 2010 VBA Date and Time Formulas

This book is about Excel 2010 Visual Basic for Applications for Dates and Times. It is a dump of codes that are useful for assignments, practice and in the work place. You will need a basic understanding of editing VBA code to find this book helpful. Standard Copyright ©, by William Smith, 2015-05-19.

Contents

Excel VBA Introduction

Shortcuts

Alt F11 = Open VB Editor
Alt F8 = Open Macros

Create a macro

Code:

```
Sub Macroname()
End Sub
```

To run a macro within another macro

Code:

```
Submittal()
Call Submittal
End Sub
```

Add comments

'This is a comment. You have to add an apostrophe before the comment.

Excel VBA Dates and Times

Date Add 53 Weeks message box
Code:

Sub Date_Add_53_Weeks()

This is a date add macro to add 53 weeks to the current date.
The date will be displayed on the message box.

MsgBox (DateAdd("ww", 53, Now))

msgbox is used to display message box
dateadd is used to add intervals to the date specified
'"ww" means add the intervals in weeks.
'53 means add 53 weeks.
Now means add intervals from today's date and time.

End Sub

Date add days macro message box

Code:

```
Sub date_add_days_macro()

On Error Resume Next

MsgBox (DateAdd("d", InputBox("Please enter
number of days to add", 1), Now))
```

msgbox means message box will be displayed
dateadd means add number of interval dates to the
date specified.
Inputbox is where the total number of days to add will
be inserted
'"d" means add days to the date specified
'Now means use today's date and time
I added 12 days to the current date which has
displayed the date in 12 days.
'the date in 12 days being the 18th.
End Sub

Figure 1 Excel VBA Date Add Days

Date add years macro message box
Code:

```
Sub date_add_macro()

On Error Resume Next

To display and add 10 extra years to the current date
on a message box

MsgBox (DateAdd("yyyy", 10, Date))

'"yyyy" means numerator or amount to add should be
in years
10 means add ten "yyyy" or add ten years
Date means use the current date or today's date
End Sub
```

Figure 2 Excel VBA Date Add Years

```
Sub date_add_macro()

On Error Resume Next

MsgBox (DateAdd("yyyy", 10, Date))


End Sub
```

Date add one month
Code:

```
Sub date_add_one_month()

On Error Resume Next

ActiveCell.FormulaR1C1 = DateAdd("m", 1,
"01/01/2013")
```

To display the date one month from the 1st of Jan
2013.
The formula value will be inserted to the current,
selected or active cell.

```
End Sub
```

Figure 3 Date Add Month

Date add one quarter message box
Code:

Sub date_add_one_quarter()

To display and add 3 months or one quarter to the current date within message box.

On Error Resume Next

MsgBox (DateAdd("q", 1, Now))

'"q" equals quarter, 1 equals one quarter, now equals today's date and time.
'today's date is 01.01.2013

End Sub

Figure 4 Excel VBA Date Add Quarter

Date value macro message box

This displays the current date in a message box.

Code:

```
Sub date_value_macro()

'To display the current date (dd/mm/yyyy) in a
message box.

On Error Resume Next

MsgBox (DateValue(Now))

End Sub
```

Figure 5 Excel VBA Date Value

```
Sub date_value_macro()

'To display the current date (dd/mm/yyyy) in a message box.

On Error Resume Next

MsgBox (DateValue(Now))

End Sub
```

15

Date Serial

The code below inserts the current date, into the selected cell in excel.

Code:

```
Sub Insert_Date_Serial()

'Comment: Date function

'Comment: Inserting the current date using the Date
Serial function

On Error Resume Next

ActiveCell.FormulaR1C1 = DateSerial(Year(Date),
Month(Date), Day(Date))

End Sub
```

Figure 6 Excel VBA Date Serial

```
Sub Insert_Date_Serial()

'Comment: Date function

'Comment: Inserting the current date using the Date Serial function

On Error Resume Next

ActiveCell.FormulaR1C1 = DateSerial(Year(Date), Month(Date), Day(Date))

End Sub
```

17

Date

The formula below will insert the current date in whichever cell is highlighted

Code:

```
Sub Insert_Date()

On Error Resume Next

ActiveCell.FormulaR1C1 = Date

End Sub
```

Figure 7 Excel VBA Date

Weekday

Enters the weekday number of the week based on the current date, Sunday being 1st day
As the day of the week is currently Tuesday, the number 3 was inputted
The weekday function is inserted in the highlighted or active cell

Code:

```
Sub Insert_Weekday_Function()

On Error Resume Next

ActiveCell.FormulaR1C1 = Weekday(Date, vbSunday)

End Sub
```

Figure 8 Excel VBA Weekday

Year

The code below inserts the current year into the selected cell in excel when run.

Code:

```
Sub year_function()

On Error Resume Next

ActiveCell.FormulaR1C1 = Year(Now())

End Sub
```

Figure 9 Excel VBA Year

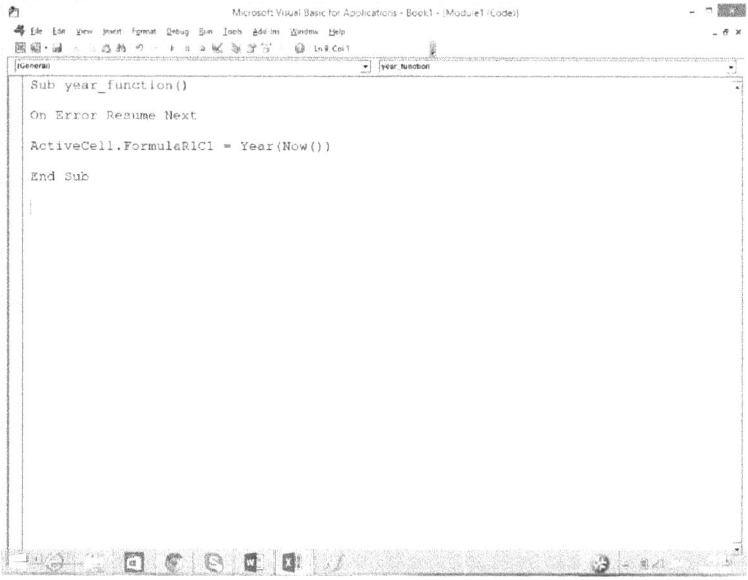

Microsoft Visual Basic for Applications - Book1 - [Module1 (Code)]
(General)
year_function
Sub year_function()
On Error Resume Next
ActiveCell.FormulaR1C1 = Year(Now())
End Sub

Day

The below code inserts the current dates Day of the month into the selected cell in excel. E.G. 22.

Code:

```
Sub day_()

On Error Resume Next

ActiveCell.FormulaR1C1 = Day(Now())

End Sub
```

Figure 10 Excel VBA Day

Hour

The code above enters the hour value of the date and time value into the selected cell in excel. E.G. 9.

Code:

```
Sub Hour_()

On Error Resume Next

ActiveCell.FormulaR1C1 = Hour(Now())

End Sub
```

Figure 11 Excel VBA Hour

```
Sub Hour_()

On Error Resume Next

ActiveCell.FormulaR1C1 = Hour(Now())

End Sub
```

Minute

The code above enters the minute value of the date and time value into the selected cell in excel. E.G. 16.

Code:

Sub Minute_()

On Error Resume Next

ActiveCell.FormulaR1C1 = Minute(Now())

End Sub

Figure 12 Excel VBA Minute

```
Sub Minute_()

On Error Resume Next

ActiveCell.FormulaR1C1 = Minute(Now())

End Sub
```

Month

The code above enters the month value of the date and time value into the selected cell in excel. E.G. 11.

Code:

```
Sub Month_()

On Error Resume Next

ActiveCell.FormulaR1C1 = Month(Now())

End Sub
```

Figure 13 Excel VBA Month

```
Sub Month_()

On Error Resume Next

ActiveCell.FormulaR1C1 = Month(Now())

End Sub
```

Second

The code above enters the second value of the date and time value into the selected cell in excel. E.G. 34.

Code:

```
Sub Second_()

On Error Resume Next

ActiveCell.FormulaR1C1 = Second(Now())

End Sub
```

Figure 14 Excel VBA Seconds

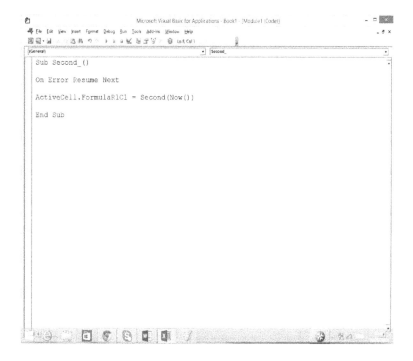

Time Value

The code below enters the current time value of the date and time value into the selected cell in excel. E.G. 10:27:18 AM.

Code:

```
Sub TimeValue_()

On Error Resume Next

ActiveCell.FormulaR1C1 = TimeValue(Now())

End Sub
```

Figure 15 Excel VBA Time Value

Message box Day of month as a number

Code:

```
Sub vba_day_of_month_as_a__number()

On Error Resume Next

MsgBox (Day(Now))

End Sub
```

The code above displays the current day of the month as a number in the message box.

Figure 16 Excel VBA Day of Month as a number

MyDateDiff function
Code:

Function MyDateDiff()

On Error Resume Next

MyDateDiff = MsgBox(DateDiff("ww", Now,
"01/01/2034", vbSunday, vbFirstJan1))

End Function

MyDateDiff function calculates the difference in weeks
(ww) between_
-today's date (Now) and the 1st of Jan 2034_
vbSunday will the assigned the first day of the week.
vbFirstJan1 will assign the 1st of Jan as the first day
of the year.

Figure 17 Excel VBA Date Difference in Weeks

Date Difference in months

Code:

```
Sub DateDifferenceMacroMnths()

On Error Resume Next

Dim e As Date

On Error Resume Next

Dim f As Date

On Error Resume Next

e = InputBox("Enter start date as dd/mm/yyyy format")

On Error Resume Next

f = InputBox("Enter end date as dd/mm/yyyy format")

On Error Resume Next

MsgBox (DateDiff("M", e, f, vbSunday, vbFirstJan1))

End Sub
```

DateDifferenceMacroMnths Macro

This macro will calculate the difference in months between two dates inputted.

"M" means calculation in months.

DateDiff means the difference between two dates.
E equals the first input box.
F equals the second input box.
VBSunday means start counting the week from Sunday.
VBFirstJan1 means the first day of the year for the calculation is the 1st of Jan.
Dim e as date means declare the input box equal to e as a date field.
Dim f as date means declare the input box equal to f as a date field.

Figure 18 Excel VBA Date Difference in months

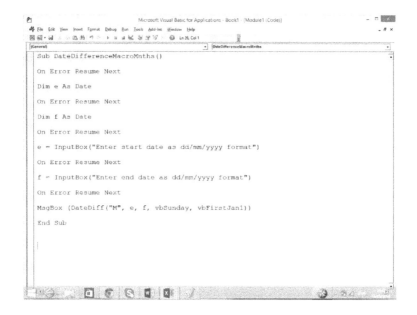

```
Sub DateDifferenceMacroMnths()

On Error Resume Next

Dim e As Date

On Error Resume Next

Dim f As Date

On Error Resume Next

e = InputBox("Enter start date as dd/mm/yyyy format")

On Error Resume Next

f = InputBox("Enter end date as dd/mm/yyyy format")

On Error Resume Next

MsgBox (DateDiff("M", e, f, vbSunday, vbFirstJan1))

End Sub
```

Date Difference Quarters

The following code calculates the difference in the number of quarters between one date and another. The dates are defined as input boxes declared as e and f. The start date is declared as e = input box... and the end date is defined as f = input box... The results are displayed in a message box.

Code:

```
Sub date_difference_quarters()

On Error Resume Next

Dim e As Date

On Error Resume Next

Dim f As Date

On Error Resume Next

e = InputBox("Enter Start Date")

On Error Resume Next

f = InputBox("Enter end date")

On Error Resume Next

MsgBox (DateDiff("q", e, f, vbSunday, vbFirstJan1))

On Error Resume Next
End Sub
```

Figure 19 Excel VBA Date Difference in Quarters

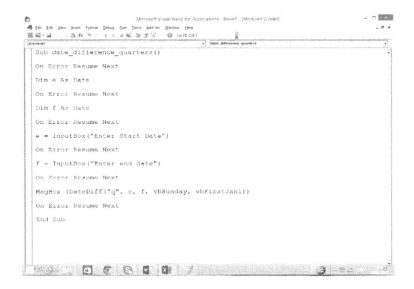

Date Difference in weeks

The following code calculates the difference in the number of weeks between one date and another. The dates are defined as input boxes declared as startdate and enddate. The start date is declared as startdate = input box… and the end date is defined as enddate = input box…The results are displayed in a message box.

Code:

```
Sub date_diff_weeks()

On Error Resume Next

Dim startdate As Date

On Error Resume Next

Dim enddate As Date

On Error Resume Next

startdate = InputBox("Enter start date")

On Error Resume Next

enddate = InputBox("Enter end date")

On Error Resume Next

MsgBox (DateDiff("ww", startdate, enddate,
        vbSunday, vbFirstJan1))

On Error Resume Next

End Sub
```

Figure 20 Excel VBA Date Difference in Weeks

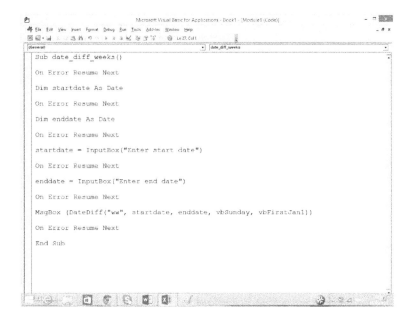

```
Sub date_diff_weeks()

On Error Resume Next

Dim startdate As Date

On Error Resume Next

Dim enddate As Date

On Error Resume Next

startdate = InputBox("Enter start date")

On Error Resume Next

enddate = InputBox("Enter end date")

On Error Resume Next

MsgBox (DateDiff("ww", startdate, enddate, vbSunday, vbFirstJan1))

On Error Resume Next

End Sub
```

Date Difference in days

The following code calculates the difference in the number of days between one date and another. The dates are defined as input boxes declared as startdate and enddate. The start date is declared as startdate = input box... and the end date is defined as enddate = input box... The results are displayed in a message box.

Code:

```vb
Sub date_diff_days()

On Error Resume Next

Dim startdate As Date

On Error Resume Next

Dim enddate As Date

On Error Resume Next

startdate = InputBox("Please enter start date")

On Error Resume Next

enddate = InputBox("Please enter end date")

On Error Resume Next

MsgBox (DateDiff("d", startdate, enddate, vbSunday, vbFirstJan1))

On Error Resume Next

End Sub
```

Figure 21 Excel VBA Date Difference in Days

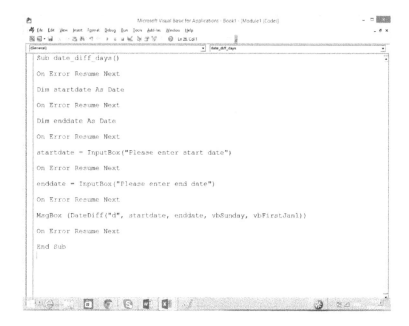

DatePart Year, show part of a date calculation

The Date Part function is used to display a specific part of a date value. In this case the program below is used to display the year "part" of the current date. "date_part_year()" is the name that has been given to the macro. "MsgBox" stands for message box. The "DatePart" bit tells the editor that you are about to enter a date part or "show part of a date" calculation. This is followed by the year symbol ("YYYY") to specify that you want to extract the year from the date. This is followed by the date value specified which in my case is "Now" standing for the current date and time. This is followed by vbSunday which tells the program that you want to select Sunday as the first day of the week. This is lastly followed by vbFirstJan1 which is used to specify the starting week of the year you want to use.

Every macro begins with the keyword "Sub" and ends with the keywords "End Sub".

Theory:

DatePart("year symbol", the Date, specific start day of week, specific start week of the year))

Code:

```
Sub date_part_year()

On Error Resume Next

MsgBox (DatePart("yyyy", Now, vbSunday,
vbFirstJan1))

On Error Resume Next

End Sub
```

Figure 22 Excel VBA Date Part Year

Date Part Month, show part of a date calculation

The Date Part function is used to display a specific part of a date value. In this case the program below is used to display the month "part" of the current date. "vba_date_part_month()" is the name that has been given to the macro. "MsgBox" stands for message box. The "DatePart" bit tells the editor that you are about to enter a date part or "show part of a date" calculation. This is followed by the month symbol ("m") to specify that you want to extract the month from the date. This is followed by the date value specified which in my case is "Now" standing for the current date and time. This is followed by vbSunday which tells the program that you want to select Sunday as the first day of the week. This is lastly followed by vbFirstJan1 which is used to specify the starting week of the year you want to use.

Every macro begins with the keyword "Sub" and ends with the keywords "End Sub".

Theory:

DatePart("month symbol", the Date, specific start day of week, specific start week of the year))

Code:

```
Sub vba_date_part_month()

On Error Resume Next

MsgBox (DatePart("m", Now, vbSunday, vbFirstJan1))

On Error Resume Next

End Sub
```

Figure 23 Excel VBA Date Part Month

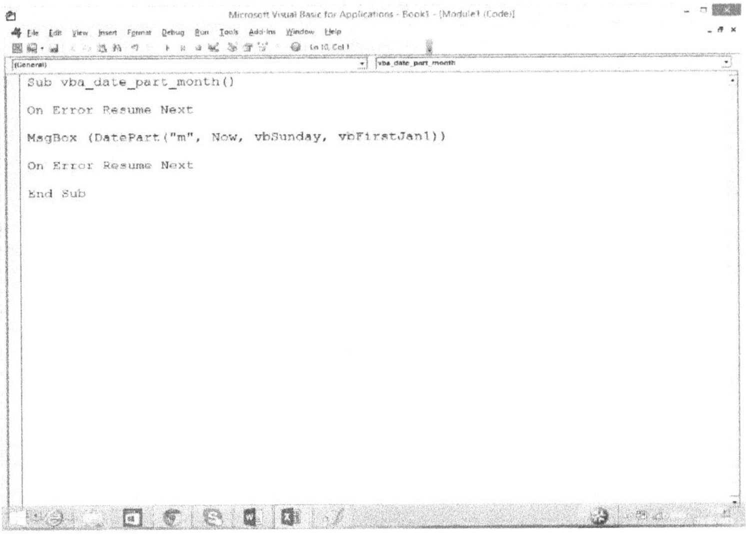

```
Sub vba_date_part_month()

On Error Resume Next

MsgBox (DatePart("m", Now, vbSunday, vbFirstJan1))

On Error Resume Next

End Sub
```

Date Part Day, show part of a date calculation

The Date Part function is used to display a specific part of a date value. In this case the program below is used to display the day "part" of the current date. "vba_date_part_Day()" is the name that has been given to the macro. "MsgBox" stands for message box. The "DatePart" bit tells the editor that you are about to enter a date part or "show part of a date" calculation. This is followed by the day symbol ("d") to specify that you want to extract the day from the date. This is followed by the date value specified which in my case is "Now" standing for the current date and time. This is followed by vbSunday which tells the program that you want to select Sunday as the first day of the week. This is lastly followed by vbFirstJan1 which is used to specify the starting week of the year you want to use.

Every macro begins with the keyword "Sub" and ends with the keywords "End Sub".

Theory:

DatePart("day symbol", the Date, specific start day of week, specific start week of the year))

Code:

```
Sub vba_date_part_Day()

On Error Resume Next

MsgBox (DatePart("d", Now, vbSunday, vbFirstJan1))

On Error Resume Next

End Sub
```

Figure 24 Excel VBA Date Part Day

```
Sub vba_date_part_Day()

On Error Resume Next

MsgBox (DatePart("d", Now, vbSunday, vbFirstJan1))

On Error Resume Next

End Sub
```

Conclusion

I suggest using the VBA help function to get more insight on how to develop a piece of code if you have not created one before. I also suggest recording macros first and then developing them further by editing them in the VBA editor.

References

Microsoft Excel 2010 VBA Help Function